A Place That Knows You

A Place That Knows You

Tiwaladeoluwa Adekunle

Etchings Press
Indianapolis, Indiana

This publication is made possible by funding provided by the Shaheen College of Arts and Sciences and the Department of English at the University of Indianapolis. Special thanks to the students who judged, edited, designed, and published this chapbook: Adam Lourenco Fernandes and Emma Knaack.

UNIVERSITY *of* INDIANAPOLIS

Published by Etchings Press
1400 E. Hanna Ave.
Indianapolis, Indiana 46227
All rights reserved

etchings.uindy.edu
www.uindy.edu/cas/english

Printed by IngramSpark

Published in the United States of America

ISBN 978-1-955521-08-6
26 25 24 23 22   1 2 3 4 5

Cover image by Tiwaladeoluwa Adekunle
Cover design by Adam Lourenco Fernandes
Interior design by Emma Knaack

Table of Contents

The past tense of country

is when you leave
your own on purpose
and fracture
your name on purpose
and yield
your accent on purpose
and measure love
and halve joy
and swallow
indignities with thanks
and flail
as the bloated belly
of memories rise to the surface

Preface

The candle last week caused a small fire
but this one burns like it should, melts as the night
stretches, into the hard concrete of a home we will never
    forget.

You are 8 and I am 5
all we know is soil and fiction,
parents who give their all and teach us to want less.

We live in a world we cannot see yet
our girlish bodies swaddled in soft cotton that will remain,
long after we ourselves

have been flung into the mouth of a beast
to eat the meat from between its teeth.

You tell me go back to your country

Like it was your idea first   this soft chorus
my body knows by heart

I have travelled the earth counterclockwise   barefoot
    a thing plucked
in search of another house with windows
    rooms that know my name

go back to your country

but my body said it first

after I forgot
the last time I said my name without *say that again*
                                        split it let me see
                                        ooh

after brittany said
my hair had been *conquered* by conditioner   a compliment

conquered   broken
  in half   like history

go back to your country

sometimes I think I have
and then I wake up to the piercing breeze in my body

the bruise of all the years of trying
to retrieve from the balled fist that is America
a golden coin

Self-Portraits in Water

i.   I am 5 years old and I bring my mother water in
          quantities that would quench
          my thirst but not hers. Bathing, I have forgotten again to
             wash my back.
          My mother refills her glass. She cleans my back. She tells
             me children
          always forget. *They think all they see is all there is.*

ii.   I am 8 and I am not allowed to look into the well for long,
          or even, my father says,
          at all. Someone tells me the water pulls children.
          They don't know how deep to look, when to turn
          around and leave.

          I look because now I must. My reflection glides upon the
             dark
          surface of the water, echoes back at me. I am not pulled,
          I think. I do not *want.*

iii.   I am 15 and my heart, flesh and frantic pounds
          against my bedroom floor. Outside, melting snow, the
             girl
          who has just yelled, from a moving car, red hair whipping
          her oval face,   *nigger!*

iv.   I lean my body against the wet wall. The water is so hot it
             scalds
          my back. I choose this. I am never
          again scrubbing just dirt.

v.   I am 19. When I think of home, I think of water
stretching endlessly, stretching regardless
clear   azure   audacious
holding continents like drifting siblings.

And if I could, wouldn't I swim the length of here
    to there?

Wouldn't I pretend *there* is not itself
        a flailing thing?

I once held in my other hand:

my milk teeth. money for lunch. a blade. a fear of doing
wrong. the way the sun shines on accra. a fear of things
being taken back. all the things I found instead of someone
else like me. nostalgia. a filmmaker on the internet who
asked me at 14, not to love him back. a desperate desire to
begin again. the film he dedicated to me. my bewilderment.
a caution around mirrors. the hues of my blindness. vomit.
my adolescent restlessness. the way it rains on ibadan.
a desperate desire to be good. the joy of knowing one
home. unripe pawpaw. the proper way to say my name.
a desperation. a desire. the way laughter echoes. the way
fear lingers. guilt. the way it warps the world.

teeth

before sore
before heavy
before learning my alone

before names
before knives
before your tongue became a knife

before silence
before I became   so   fluent

I put myself in your open mouth, said
don't bite or
the shame will not stop bleeding

said please
said please
said stop

in relief, in wonder

my mother's fingers nudge fish bones out of my throat. steady, precise. like she'd trained for my choking. any wavering from her always in the past tense. I cried last night, she'd say sometimes, always with clear, bright eyes, any sadness, a wisp caught in the past. she, already dancing again. her chiffon voice, swirling around me, a soft breeze on the wounds I hid from places I should never have gone. and where wouldn't I go? what wouldn't I touch? I wanted even then, to lose myself in something. everything I was given, I dangled over a cliff. I learned about bulimia and steered my own fingers into my own throat, peered at the green-yellow chunks of food in the white bowl, repulsed, a new hunger ripening. I would try anything, go anywhere, to run from the sadness that woke in me. after months of contemplation, I would tell her I was ready to leave my body. and she would ask why. and then tell me why not. and I would believe her. steady. precise. as if she'd trained for my choking. I wake up on dark mornings to her singing. in my nightmares, she fights on my side. I rest the weight of my head on her one palm. tears running down my face, then her arm. in relief. in wonder.

A Smaller Joy

Moving fish from the river years ago, one leaped out of our
    bucket
unto the hot concrete, slipped out of our hands as we tried to
    place it
again in the bucket, where it could live.

I've wondered since, how do you move a thing alive, from
one joy to a smaller joy?

Last year, I could almost, but not quite remember
how to love you—the way one might almost, but not quite,
    remember
the parts of a song. My love for you had leaped out its place
in my body, where it could live.

I would say the words, like you might hum the lyrics you
    remember,
but feel nothing—this was the first sadness to carry—

it weighed so little, I was glad—this was the second sadness.

Soft-Spoken

I speak decibels lower than I should like Daisy
from The Great Gatsby; I do it in hopes
that people hear nothing;

some might call this a way to survive; I knead
silence mid-sentence (offer it, grasp it);
my words teeter into nothing;

In the midst of a clause, I consider rocks
again; are they silent or silenced;
heavy, but with the weight of saying nothing;

In the bend of a phrase, I imagine earth unfurling
in my fist; my breath catches;
no one knows if I'm soft or if I'm fading to nothing.

nickname

it glints like tinsel in her mouth
an offering she calls a solution
we americans lose our attention span after the first two syllables

I pause for a moment
my throat grips itself

and then I join her laughter

a non-exhaustive list of pros and cons for loving you

cons

i. you have little respect for boundaries
ii. you say you've learned from your past but you still do
    awful things
iii. i've seen what you do to girls like me
iv. you cannot spell my name
v. you do not love me back

pros

(but tell me, america, what is more american than
claiming something whether it wants you or not?)

mother tongue

I can't say mother tongue in my mother tongue

i.   mother tongue, I hope you taste the fear
        that soaks my tongue when I search
               for a word and it   eludes me
        when I look and you are not
        behind me

        fear, because if I lose you
        in what language
        shall I call you back?

ii.   mother always said: *I will speak to you in Yoruba*
        but you
        must respond in english

        mother let me dance but not sing
        she was preparing me for the world
        we are enough she says, but no one else agrees

iii.   mother tongue, know
        that when I break, truly break, I
        break into you, your heavy chords teaching
        my bones carefulness

        and how can I not know it when
        your melody is so precise
        the world *aye* can become space *aaye*
        in one wrong turn?

iv.   I write this in english, but you are always here
my words wear the wind from home like perfume
so they always know
I am not theirs

v.   soul song, trunk
if I lose you I will find you
if you run
I will run too

ode to my h-factor

you

hiccup
abit of history
losing and finding the letter *h*
placing it heverywhere but ere

hum
eirloom
heat that rises from a smoldering alf
inch of air under my tongue

haze
ourmony
iss of resistance
telling everyone who cares to ear:

here is how hard it is to bear english,
here is how far i will go, and no lower

Homecoming

busy as it is weaving
the logics that hold one life,
a good body is one that wakes up,
everything else is a gift.

I've learned to forgive the betrayals of my own
I've returned to it like a country I left in a hurry,
where everything has changed but the soul.

I only have left, the leaving

I have not forgotten
your embrace, your grace, your flag a brazen
shawl around my frame. It takes nothing
to bring it all back. Only yesterday, Paramore.
Williams' strawberry pink hair and silvery voice:
After all this time, I'm still into you

You. Over a decade, still I dream you. One song and the
    stars are
again silver buttons on the velvet sky. The glistening
dust films my feet, my infant face peers back at me
from the dark surface of the pond.

since I left you, should I not leave you?

Too late now. I've fallen in love with longing. Its bloated
    belly
of memories. How it feels to trace the breadth of the
    thousand
miles between here and there. To transplant in poem
the backyard tree. To haul it across the ocean.

No, I cannot leave you.
I gape through the window at your doors
I dig my feet into the ground, I place my hands against
your walls, soft as skin, swollen
with salt water.

Acknowledgements

Thank you to Etchings Press for nurturing this work.

I would like to thank the editors of the following publications, for publishing some of the poems included: *Breakwater Review*, *Oakland Review*, and *2017 Best "New" African Poets*.

Thank you Esther Edoho, Tolu Oloruntoba, and Tomi Olugbemi for your gracious and generous critique of these poems. They would not exist in this form without you.

Thank you mum and dad for your unrelenting love and support. I am forever grateful to be your daughter.

Thank you to my siblings, for your love, prayers, generosity, and genetleness. I love you all.

Joshua, thank you for enduring all the terible first drafts. Thank you for being my very best friend. I love you forever.

Thank you God, for calling me Beloved, and helping me to believe it. I love You too.

Colophon

Interior text is set in Source Serif 4 Subhead. Cover text is set in Rift.

About Etchings Press

Etchings Press is a student-run publisher at the University of Indianapolis that runs a post-publication award—the Whirling Prize—as well as an annual publication contest for one poetry chapbook, one prose chapbook, and one novella. On occasion, Etchings Press publishes new chapbooks from previous winners. For more information about these contests and the Whirling Prize post-publication award, please visit etchings.uindy.edu.

Previous winners and publications:

Poetry
2022: *A Place That Knows You*
    by Tiwaladeoluwa Adekunle
2022: *The Vaudeville Horse* by Elizabeth Kerlikowske
2021: *My Mother's Ghost Scrubs the Floor at 2 a.m.*
    by Robert Okaji
2020: *Vaginas Need Air* by Tori Grant Welhouse
2019: *As Lovers Always Do* by Marne Wilson
2018: *In the Herald of Improbable Misfortunes*
    by Robert Campbell
2017: *Uncle Harold's Maxwell House Haggadah*
    by Danny Caine
2016: *Some Animals* by Kelli Allen
2015: *Velocity of Slugs* by Joey Connelly
2014: *Action at a Distance* by Christopher Petruccelli

Prose
2022: *Triple Point* by Laura Story Johnson (essays)
2021: Bad Man Love Stories by Curtis VanDonkelaar
(fiction)
2020: Three in the Morning and You Don't Smoke Anymore
   by Peter J. Stavros (fiction)
2019: Dissenting Opinion from the Committee for the
   Beatitudes by Marc J. Sheehan (fiction)
2018: *The Forsaken* by Chad V. Broughman (fiction)
2017: *Unravelings* by Sarah Cheshire (memoir)
2016: *Pathetic* by Shannon McLeod (essays)
2015: *Ologies* by Chelsea Biondolillo (essays)
2014: *Static: Stories* by Frederick Pelzer (fiction)

Novella
2022: *Goodbye to the Ocean* by Susan L. Lin
2021: *Miss Alma May Learns to Fight* by Stuart Rose
2020: *Under Black Leaves* by Doug Ramspeck
2019: *Savonne, Not Vonny* by Robin Lee Lovelace
2018: *Edge of the Known Bus Line* by James R. Gapinski
2017: *The Denialist's Almanac of American Plague*
   and Pestilence by Christopher Mohar
2016: *Followers* by Adam Fleming Petty

Chapbooks from Previous Winners
2022: *slighted.* by Chad V. Broughman (fiction)
2020: *Fruit Rot* by James R. Gapinski (fiction)
2016: *#LOVESONG* by Chelsea Biondolillo (microessays
with photos and found text)

Author Biography

Tiwaladeoluwa Adekunle's poems appear in *Breakwater Review, Indiana Review, Oakland Review,* and *Pittsburg Poetry Journal*, among others. She has been nominated for a Best of the Net prize and a Pushcart prize. She was born in southwestern Nigeria.